Friedrich Hölderlin's
Life, Poetry and Madness

Published by Hesperus Press

Hesperus Press Limited

28 Mortimer Street,

London, W1W 7RD

www.hesperuspress.com

First published in German 1831

This translation first published by Hesperus Press Limited, 2018

Introduction and English language translation by

© Will Stone 2018

Edited by Linden Lawson

Designed and typeset by Roland Codd

Printed in Liber Duplex Barcelona

ISBN : 978-184391-597-3

Friedrich Hölderlin's
Life, Poetry and
Madness

Wilhelm Waiblinger
Translated by Will Stone

HESPERUS

Friedrich Hölderlin by
Luise Keller, 1842

Introduction

But the more perceptive man? Oh, he who began to
perceive and is silent now – exposed on the mountains
of the heart . . .

RILKE

In the Protestant Cemetery of Rome, famed as the resting
place of those 'matchless singers', the English Romantic
poets Keats and Shelley, lies another, lesser-known
Romantic of equally tender age. He is the German poet
Wilhelm Waiblinger, who was laid to rest there in January
1830 aged only twenty-five, a probable victim of syphilis.
Today Waiblinger is best known in terms of his relationship to the great German lyric poet Friedrich Hölderlin
during the latter's renowned seclusion from 1807 to
1843 in the now-named 'Hölderlinturm', the Hölderlin
Tower in Tübingen, and for the essay memoir he wrote in
1827–8 about the stricken Swabian poet, entitled *Friedrich
Hölderlins Leben, Dichtung und Wahnsinn*. Waiblinger never
saw the essay published, for it did not appear in Germany
until 1831, a year after his death.

Waiblinger, friend of another up-and-coming poet in the early 1820s, Eduard Mörike, was known as a rebel, a wayward fellow and a liberal maverick, an independent thinker. The two friends were theology students in Tübingen, in the very same Protestant seminary, the 'Tübinger Stift', where Hölderlin had studied alongside Schelling and Hegel from 1788. The young Waiblinger was naturally inclined to be anti-Establishment, to ardently follow the path of freedom, the writings he left behind fairly flash with anger and wilfully scatter their shards of disrespect; but the swashbuckling Waiblinger also happened to appear at a time when a certain frustration with the prevailing culture was already in the air. Huge movements in philosophy and poetry were afoot and Hölderlin was an instrumental figure within them before his reasoning was affected. The senior poet Hölderlin, the ultimate tortured outsider, a high-flown spirit broken by fate, doomed to a life of semi-sequestration, raving in madness at the injustices which befell him and pacing alone in a tower, must have seemed to Waiblinger like an overwhelmingly seductive subject and a dramatic portent of the sort of punishment that might await him should he not take control of his already chaotic life.

During the winter of 1827–8, after departing to Rome, Waiblinger penned what would be his historically valuable portrait of the older poet, drawn from his many visits to Hölderlin in his tower chamber in the early to mid 1820s.

These visits apparently commenced in the summer of 1822 and ended in the autumn of 1826, roughly a four-year period, with the most intense series of encounters made over a year and a half through 1822–3. However, in his essay Waiblinger extends the period dramatically between last seeing Hölderlin and his departure for Italy, speaking as if he is looking back nostalgically on a distant epoch. Having encountered Hölderlin's poetry and, most importantly, a new publication of his unclassifiable novel *Hyperion*, at age seventeen, Waiblinger resolved to seek out the now fifty-two-year-old author (then considered virtual old age) or the 'Madman' as he terms him in his diary, who resided but a stone's throw away in the house of the benevolent carpenter Ernst Zimmer. His family having abandoned him, Hölderlin had been taken in by the culturally aware carpenter in 1807 after being released from the clinic of Dr Ferdinand Autenrieth in Tübingen, where he had been incarcerated since 1806 and was soon deemed incurably insane. On release the good doctors thanked Zimmer for his charitable gesture and gave his charge a mere three years to live. Zimmer had read *Hyperion* and obviously sensed something of the gravity of Hölderlin's dire position in spiritual terms, so he resolved to accommodate him and attend to his needs. Part of his house beside the River Neckar contained a tower which had formerly been a defensive stronghold within the city walls. Here a simply furnished room on the first floor became home to the estranged poet for the prolonged latter stage of his existence. Waiblinger was an early visitor, one who was uniquely tolerated by the highly strung and nervous occupant of the tower. Having got over the initial horror of the spectacle of the eccentric Hölderlin before him, Waiblinger became more and more drawn to visit him, the man in the tower providing a living tragic figure onto whom he could project his own existential hopes and fears, his own preoccupation with madness and the danger of losing one's self entirely. Gradually, through repeated visits, Waiblinger could begin to amass fascinating details of the day-to-day life of this curious victim of his own hypersensitivity, fleshing out a portrait or as close to one as could be expected of the 'unfortunate' during these years of seclusion.

Waiblinger became increasingly obsessed by Hölderlin through a combination of visits and reading the newly published single edition of *Hyperion* which had appeared in 1822. Waiblinger's own attempt at a lyrical novel, *Phaeton*, from 1823 became his homage to *Hyperion*, and the hero is based around Hölderlin. In his diaries of the time, Waiblinger effuses over Hölderlin as a poet of the highest sensibility and ideals, a rare, noble mind, a mind possessed of a unique spiritual purity, whose verse proves infinitely intoxicating. On 7 August 1822 he states: 'This Hölderlin disturbs me greatly. God, God! Such thoughts, this high-born pure spirit and this mad man! *Hyperion* is saturated with spirit: A fervent fully glowing soul swells there. Nature is his true divinity. He is endlessly original, ingenious. Hölderlin is dearer to my heart than Hölty, Neuffer, Weisser, Haug, Schwab, all of them put together. Hölderlin has been sent from heaven to be a poet on earth. Hölderlin shakes me to the core. I find in him an eternally rich form of sustenance.' This sort of effusive entry continues during this period, when his reading of the elder poet is gradually forming into a mental kinship, apprentice and master. It is *Hyperion* above all which is the drug Waiblinger must have, though its potency in the end proves too much. 'I cannot read it for long, for I go under in such a sea: I am stricken with vertigo, I'm shaken to the very core . . . my brain itself is on fire . . .'

But once Waiblinger had become used to the unconventional appearance and peculiar comportment of the strange figure in the tower room, he also began to feel genuine affection for the 'Madman' on a personal level, as comrades and fellow mavericks, as outsiders beyond the Establishment. But Waiblinger is still positioned on the living side of the Styx whilst Hölderlin had already been ferried across by Charon, but was now caught on a sandbank midway. Waiblinger may appear the sane, the scientific, the safe one, rooted in robust life, surveying the wreckage of Hölderlin from the gilded towers of Rome, but unknown to himself he is a marked man and has but months to live. The tragedy awaiting Waiblinger as he writes his memoir invests the piece with even greater pathos. The essay exhibits both the attempt to discuss Hölderlin's spiritual decline in abstract scientific terms, from a detached observer's point of view as it were, employing a philosophic, reflective tone, as well as through a more personal compassionate humanistic approach. Waiblinger, who was a rather unrestrained bohemian character and self-confessedly showed signs of mental strife himself (most often manifesting through the imbalance in his attitudes towards established literary figures), found in the fallen Hölderlin a human subject suffering likewise but on a higher level around whom his own Romantic idealisation and directionless spiritual intoxication could be bridled. Hölderlin was a lesson, a terrifying example of the physical and mental health potentiality of imaginative thought unrestrained. But the hunched survivor spewing gibberish that Hölderlin now was, this blown husk of a once-soaring spirit, now lost to inanities, effusive bowing and peculiar eccentricities, must also have seemed to Waiblinger something eminently dramatic in itself as an individual case of human tragedy. How could it be that such a personal torment and a degradation could be thus prolonged without death as the desired cauterising dénouement, and the ultimate tantalising question raised then of a possible cure, of some miraculous future restoration of sanity, if only temporary.

Hölderlin did not welcome visitors, especially new ones – this is made plain in Waiblinger's account – so there was something about this fresh-featured, ardent young man that the reticent, suspicious Hölderlin warmed to: perhaps he saw himself as a younger man, we can but speculate. Waiblinger's gushing praise for *Hyperion* must have been a key factor in this acceptance at the outset, but as time went by Hölderlin clearly developed an interest in or liking for the younger man, or at least his presence became a reassuring convention and thus a degree of mutual trust and expectation were established. One of the most moving sections of the essay concerns the walks the two made to Waiblinger's rented summer residence, the Pressel garden house, romantically positioned on the Österberg above Tübingen. That Waiblinger even managed to persuade the notoriously unco-operative Hölderlin to accompany him such a distance was an impressive feat, which those who cared for the poet and were used to his intransigence were at pains to comprehend. And we are told that even after Waiblinger had left the vicinity, Hölderlin, on his walks with the carpenter's daughters into the fields and meadows around the town, would still approach the garden house, knock on the door and enquire of Herr Waiblinger's whereabouts. Through his regular comings and goings, Waiblinger appears to have been attempting to improve Hölderlin's lot, almost administering a benign therapy of sorts. We hear how he listens to him read, tries to give him books, patiently endures his excruciatingly repetitive piano-playing, suffering the ghoulish clickety clack of his uncut nails passing back and forth across the keys, points out subjects of interest in the landscape, joins him in a conspiratorial smoke and the imbibing of wine and beer. Waiblinger seeks to bring this pained, disturbed and dysfunctional man back to some remembrance of normality, to make out the distant echoes of social inter-action. Waiblinger is caught in a web of fascination for the tower man: a powerful mixture of pity, revulsion, fervour and admiration brings him back again and again.

The first visit Waiblinger made to the tower is recounted in his diary as being on 3 July 1822. These diary entries shadow much of the 'action' which takes place in the essay itself, as if such moments were recalled from the diary and then fleshed out further as memoir. On this initial excursion to the carpenter's house Waiblinger was accompanied by his friend Wurm. The pretext was to request a certain poem by Hölderlin. Waiblinger's account tells how they descended the stone steps to the bank of the Neckar and approached a large house before which lay the tools and materials of the carpenter, confirming it was the right address. Climbing a staircase, they were met by one of the carpenter's daughters, a 'gorgeous girl' whom Waiblinger was immediately besotted with, who asked them what they wanted there. But before they could offer a reply the door opened and they looked in on a small,

12

spartan, circular room with meagre furnishings. Within the figure of a man stood half dressed, washing his hands. This 'terrible form' proved such a shock to Waiblinger that he was cast into a state of confusion, but he managed to gather himself, advanced and politely explained his purpose. Hölderlin looked Waiblinger over with a gaze which, he asserted, sent a cold shiver through the young man's innards. His friend Wurm appeared to be less fazed. Hölderlin then began to pour forth compliments, addressed Waiblinger as 'Your Royal Majesty' and made a series of inarticulate or incomprehensible sounds seemingly peppered with French. He also bowed deeply. The pair of visitors were taken aback, fell silent, but the girl behind them urged them to press on, to talk to him further as they loitered undecided in the doorway. Hölderlin suddenly murmured out of the blue, 'I am now about to become a Catholic, your Royal Majesty.' Wurm then tried another tack – to interest him in the current affairs of the Greeks, since Hölderlin had famously held a burning passion for Greece in his former life – but he merely showered the pair with further compliments and gave forth a stream of incomprehensible words, saying, 'Your Royal Majesty, on that subject I am unable to answer.' The single comprehensible exchange concerned the impressive view from the window opposite across the river. 'Yes, yes, beautiful, beautiful, your Royal Majesty, Royal Lords.' The two, having used up their reserves of niceties and patience, hastened from the room, then after five minutes or so chatting with the carpenter they departed the house.

Following this bizarre experience, Waiblinger professes to have thought of nothing else but Hölderlin and also, tellingly, of the beautiful young girl and when he might see her again. Later Waiblinger returns to his accounts of further visits, recounting how, on a visit on 22 February 1823, Hölderlin played the piano incessantly, how his playing lasted for an incredible eight days in a row and how he continued during Waiblinger's visit as if he were not even there. On a visit of 9 June he is rebuffed, for the poet is prostrate in bed and makes excuses, bidding his 'Royal Majesty' to leave. The carpenter mysteriously informs Waiblinger of 'how even masturbation contributes to the poet's reveries'. Now Hölderlin recognises the younger poet on his visits and addresses him not only as 'Your Majesty' but also as 'Your Holiness', 'Your Grace', 'Your Excellency', even 'The Lord Father'. When enquiring of Hölderlin's age, Waiblinger is met with a barrage of French vocabulary. One day in July 1823 Hölderlin is reading from his *Hyperion* before the window in the Pressel garden house. Waiblinger gushes: 'Oh I am still a child in joy. Hölderlin is my dearest friend! He is only insane . . .'; and later, in a letter to Uhland on 7 July 1823: 'This lunatic, sitting at the window of my garden house, well I can tell you he is far closer to me than the thousands out there who are said to be sane.' The following year Waiblinger's diary entries become increasingly cryptic, and the references to Hölderlin cease altogether after the late summer of 1824. In February 1826, however, in a letter to one Müllner, he speaks of Hölderlin and his special circumstance of coming to know the poet better than most and fearing the prospect of someone else's potentially 'superficial' account, all but formally announcing his own work which he will set down in Rome two years later.

The publishing of Waiblinger's memoir of the poet in the Tübingen Tower led to a renewed interest in Hölderlin in the years following the author's early death, and further accounts in succeeding years tended to draw on or steal from Waiblinger's pioneering work. The poignancy of Waiblinger's memories of his time spent with Hölderlin is evident, but there has been controversy over the true purpose of Waiblinger's account, partly due to the latter's reputation as a rebel in Tübingen, a serial womaniser and sometime drunkard. This once-wild man of letters attempted to explain and justify his behaviour and state of mind later from Rome, when he had time to reflect on his excesses, to show that he had reformed, that he was no longer prone to madness like his subject. This is why the account has an air of paternal reprimand about it especially towards the beginning, when for example he suggests things might have gone differently for Hölderlin had he retained a sense of humour. But later this mild hen-pecking morphs into a comradely gentleness as the reader sees the true sympathetic relationship between the young poet and his eccentric charge gradually emerge like a winter sun appearing hopefully through dull cloud.

When Waiblinger died in Rome, Hölderlin still had another twelve years to while away in the emptiness of his tower room. He had been a resident in the carpenter Zimmer's house for thirty-six years. Following Waiblinger's departure and the publication of his account, Hölderlin became more and more a target of curiosity-seekers and autograph-hunters. Visitors would seek out the mad poet in the tower and depart, having heard a long-winded performance of piano music, or victoriously clutching one of the spontaneous myriad verses Hölderlin churned out for such individuals, bearing fictitious dates and in the last years the Italianate signature he had ascribed to himself, 'Scardanelli', and also on occasion 'Salvator Rosa'. One cannot help but recall here the similar delusional signatures of the later Nietzsche in his madness as he signed himself 'Dionysus' or 'the Crucified One', but also Maupassant and his use of the aristocratic 'Maufrigneuse', after being sent mad by the effects of syphilitic illness.

The human tragedy of Hölderlin's pathetic situation over these decades seems shocking to us, recalling in some sense the even more squalid fate of Mozart, for example, given the prestigious position Hölderlin enjoys today in the realm of German letters and in world poetry. His own family abandoned him and did all they could to avoid contributing to his upkeep. His mother never visited him at the tower, and after her death in 1828 sibling rivalry broke out over the will: Hölderlin's sister and stepbrother attempted to amend it so that their mad relation (who naturally remained oblivious to all) would not receive such a large portion. These grotesque machinations and the bloodless indifference shown by his relations to his fate was sealed when no one from Hölderlin's family even attended his funeral. The only mourners were the remaining Zimmer family (Zimmer had died in 1838).

Since Hölderlin had been in the tower his reputation had gradually faded in contemporary circles, and by the time of his death his work was all but ignored. His was a forgotten name. It was only later that his star began to stand out more brightly in the firmament to a new generation, when his special hymnic style, fusing Greek myth and Romantic mysticism, started to appeal to the mindset of nineteenth-century poets and thinkers, most notably Nietzsche, but also to musicians such as Schumann and Brahms. In the twentieth century his influence gained more ground as a slew of composers, including Hindemith and Britten, set his verse to music, and poets, writers and philosophers, among them Rilke, Hesse, Trakl, Benjamin, Celan and Heidegger, all proved enthusiastic disciples. It is true to say that poets such as Rilke, Trakl and Celan could not sound the way they do, could not sustain their own voice with such authority and distinction, without the indispensable precedence of Hölderlin. But all these arguably owe something also to Wilhelm Waiblinger, who was snuffed out too early, but just had time to stake his claim at the start of the Hölderlin legacy. For it was Waiblinger who, after the single edition of *Hyperion* appeared in 1822, continually voiced the need for a collection of Hölderlin's poetry to be published. Eventually his contemporaries the poets Uhland and Schwab edited the first collection in 1826. Much was left out, however, and it was not till 1842, a year before Hölderlin's death, that an expanded edition appeared. The key 'later' works written between 1800 and 1808 did not appear in Germany until just before the First World War, when in 1913 the landmark six-volume 'Berlin edition' was finally published by Norbert von Hellingrath, who fell at Verdun in 1916. This was followed by the Sophocles and Pindar translations. It was no coincidence that around this time Rilke was writing his famous *Duino Elegies*, which of course owe so much to Hölderlin's own later hymns and elegies. Today, rival modern editions have been able to show the full chronological trajectory of Hölderlin's works and the whole gamut of variants and fragments hitherto absent, allowing the reader a window onto the panorama of Hölderlin's vision, where the ebb and flow of lyrical dynamism and suspension can be fully appreciated.

Wilhelm Waiblinger died in Rome in the winter of 1831, his psychological study of Hölderlin as yet unpublished. He had resisted the notion of Hölderlin being simply mad, for Waiblinger suggested that this was a spirit merely exhausted, foundering, having lost its way, suggesting there might be a way back, while Zimmer, close by and long observing, was more succinct: 'It was the too much he had inside him that caused his mind to give way', a phrase which reminds us of Rilke's take on Trakl. 'He succumbed to the unbearable weight of his own existence.' But, crucially, Waiblinger apparently believed that despite the acute and chronic diagnosis there was still hope, hope that at some future point a temporary lull might occur and a period of reason would return to this tormented spirit. Why did Waiblinger sense this? On what evidence? Or was it just wishful thinking on his part? We cannot know. Waiblinger's account shows that, for all the further questions it poses and its inherent ambiguities seen across time, the foundation behind his literary enterprise was one of over-riding humanism and compassion. Waiblinger believed in the spirit of Hölderlin as it once was and in its corrupted state, and he was driven to write what he did from the distant vantage point of Rome through a growing desire to have his say and from the lingering intoxication of Hölderlin's poetry. Waiblinger sensed that he and he alone was in the best position to reveal the poet who had either unknowingly or willingly lost his reason in order to separate from a world he found intolerable. But for all Waiblinger's attempts to delineate pictorially this fantastically estranged life and its ramifications, it is the following sobering quote by Hölderlin which he chooses to include that ultimately persuades: 'Only now do I understand human beings, now that I live far from them and in solitude.'

Will Stone

Friedrich Hölderlin's
Life, Poetry and Madness

A long time has passed since I resolved to tell the world something of Hölderlin's history, his former life, or rather half-life, his existence in the shadows and above all its terrible nexus, and have been inspired to do so from more than one quarter by friends of his Muse. Five long years with the unfortunate placed me above any other in the ideal position to observe him, come to know him, to explore the fantastic course of his ideas, to bring to light the causes and embryonic signs of his madness. More than anyone else I took pains to endure his moods. The handful of his former friends who bothered to pay him a visit in his now twenty years of solitude only languished but a brief moment. Either pity overcame them and the sight of this mournful spiritual decline shook them to the core, or they swiftly concluded that it was futile to exchange a single word, to waste their attention on one with such a hopelessly confused state of mind. As for me, I considered not a single hour I accorded to him wasted, visiting him as I did unceasingly for a number of years, receiving him often at my home, or accompanying him on solitary walks in the gardens and vineyards, sometimes procuring writing paper for him, leafing through his half-finished manuscripts, bringing him books, letting him read to me and encouraging him on countless occasions to play the piano and to sing. So little by little I became accustomed to him and managed to stem the horror we naturally sense in the presence of such fallen spirits, and in his way he too became accustomed to my presence, overcoming the shyness which paralysed him when amongst people with whom he was unfamiliar. I resolved then to somehow articulate the anatomy of his current mental state, to deduce in a strictly scientific manner the cause and evolution of the appalling perturbation afflicting his soul, and to pursue it from the first causes and stirrings to the point at which any sense of mental equilibrium was inexorably abandoned. Yet this resolve was all too easily left to drift owing to a hundred other ephemeral projects, in all the trials and troubles of a highly charged existence. Now that my marvellous melancholic companion is so distant from me and that the sorrowful image of the lonely one has been expunged by these luminous southern skies, I have the uncanny desire, at arm's length from my homeland, to finally accomplish my portrait. I can no longer resist the call. And though my ambition is not to indulge in some philosophical enquiry as to the nature of Hölderlin's inwardness, I shall nevertheless endeavour to share the observations and reflections which were impressed on me during our times together. It is not my place either to offer some profound psychological insight, but rather to limit the quest to simple observation, a modest character sketch which could be of service to all those who show an interest in Hölderlin, who value his Muse, those who would like to hear something a little more precise, and to learn how this troubled spirit lives now in relation to the external world. In so doing I may indulge myself in saying a few words on the poetry itself, whose loveliest blooms and ripest fruits have been finally gathered, edited and offered up to the light of the world by those two highly respected friends of the poet, Ludwig Uhland[1] and Gustav Schwab.[2] Truth be told, I don't even know if he is still alive, many years and a great distance have stood between us, and for twenty-four years now he has been cloistered, beyond contact with the world and men, so much so that he might as well be considered no longer amongst us. It will be no offence to feeling and propriety therefore if we paint a picture publicly of his current condition. For like his poetry, his life belongs to our epoch, to our homeland, to our intellect; suffice that we take care not to get too close to the unfortunate. We must respect that timid, murky reverence for the obscure power in whose grip he struggled his whole life long, whose despotic and terrifying might we encounter so often as the subject of his complaints and struggles in the works he has left us, and not form with undue haste a too generalised judgement on a spiritual phenomenon, which in the end will surely remain an enigma to us however much we may seek to rationally describe the phenomenon in all its causes and consequences.

Let us begin by speaking of the first part of his life in the external world, then seek to link this with my own observations, so that we might see how they morph into the later stages of his existence. In terms of germination, the initial causes of this woeful development must be traced back to the earliest stage of his upbringing, and especially the uniquely tragic composition of his soul which was ultimately crushed beneath the weight of the sum of sorrowful happenings, those sad constellations of external circumstances which were implicit to him alone.

Friedrich Hölderlin was born in 1770 in Nürtingen, on the River Neckar in south Germany. It appears that his upbringing was eminently good, tender, replete with love and a certain refinement. Hölderlin always retained a considerable affection for his birthplace and for his mother, who was still alive when I left Germany. This soul then was composed of an infinite delicateness, noble, fine, deep of feeling but all too sensitive, with an audacious and daring imagination, a soul in early childhood lulled with poetic reveries, but in youth progressively constructing a world in which the most bitter sufferings were perceived as the necessary creative element of inwardness, as the stark, arduously borne antithesis to the real world. This soul also enjoyed a highly developed aptitude for music and the poetic arts, gifts encouraged, nourished and sustained through the tender vigilance of his parents. Already Friedrich's appearance was lovable over most; the youthful Friedrich's face revealed an open, amicable air: his deep, glowing, beautiful eyes, both ardent and profound, a high brow, an air of reserve yet vital with spirit, seductive without being over-sweet, winning over every heart. The generosity of his soul, an innate nobleness, his warm and lively manner of thinking and feeling and that natural grace made him so likeable and his keen intelligence and stunning gifts fulfilled all the best hopes of his teachers, his friends and family. A pure sense, an immaculate virginal soul earned him respect and love. In later years he conserved these traits, as he began to create out of the same unsullied heart, the pure source of his interiority, and dedicated his life to poetry. And the purity remained even when the hard blows of fate had conspired to cause the destruction of his spirit. Hölderlin would remain pure and pristine in his gentle, almost feminine soul, in his struggle to go on, but for him untamed diversions and the dizzying intoxication of the senses could only draw him towards corruption and death. What followed has taught us this at least.

Gifted, warm-hearted, with considerate manners, a most expressive and kindly face, the young Hölderlin attracted young and old to him in equal measure. Had there been one who could guide the young man in his development following his happy youth, in a direction more suited to his desires and ambitions, his dreams and gifts, then his mind might have retained its lucidity. But as it was, things turned out very differently. Hölderlin's malign destiny led him to a seminary,[3] where young men were equipped for the study of Theology. Due to external pressure he was obliged to pursue this course of study, even though he admitted later during his period of madness that it was expressly against his natural inclinations. He would have preferred to study exclusively ancient literature, the fine arts and above all poetry, but equally philosophy and aesthetics. Perhaps it was also the manner in which the masters sought to teach languages and science that was so injurious to this impatient and gifted young man. Much might be said of these institutions, but in truth too much power is in the hands of a single teacher. We note how often such minds, although highly learned, are extremely restricted in spite of deep learning, how unclear, directionless and digressive they are in attaining their objectives, how in them all is complex, how rare it is for such a teacher to possess clear judgement, they who are, we must confess, the least equipped to guide youth, how little talent and power they expend to awaken emerging faculties, to nourish them and set them on the right path, how much these scholars remain oblivious to life and barely know anything of men.

It is not difficult, then, to see how rare talents might drift onto dangerous paths, never again able to better themselves through their own self-education, sent raving mad by these wretched autodidacts, who fatally corrupt them through narrowness of vision and sheer incompetence. Instead of having the foresight to discern the student's receptivity in terms of his own nature and adapt their teaching accordingly, they simply plough on regardless, always in the one undeviating direction, as if the student were no more than a clock whose spring is to be rewound at the whim of the teacher. This dismal experience might well then have left its stain on the already pristine and vulnerable nature of our young poet. Yet he zealously studied ancient languages, proved himself one of the best in class, and excelled in Greek.

By chance I picked up a fine little anecdote about Hölderlin from around this time. The mother of one of my friends once told him how the young, handsome and good-natured Hölderlin had a crush on her when they were barely out of childhood. In spite of his life at the Monastery,[4] out of the fervent spirit of the sixteen-year-old arose a tender flame for this young woman, who reciprocated, and so they would walk together in a charming garden. This secret affair touched his imagination at the keenest point, nourished him and filled him with those gentle emotions which so delightfully enchant and beautify youth. Hölderlin's sensibility, his nature, his very existence were heightened further by this experience, and as a consequence his nature as a whole was made more perilously refined and cosseted. His poetry, however, received from it a measure of sustenance and vitality.

All the same, his poems then were but imitations and curious efforts, showing none of the individual uniqueness of a Schiller or Klopstock who went before him.

However, the writings of his university years already bear witness to a unique character. An enthusiasm for Greek antiquity, the study of ancient Greek masterpieces left their mark on the tonality of his own creations, revealing themselves also in his later, more perfected compositions. His entire soul depended on Greece and he drank with unslaked desire at the springs of that pure beauty, at those products of the most healthy nature, the simplest mode of thought, the most grandiose ambition. Hölderlin himself was hardly a stranger to the hunger for renown, his head fairly crammed with plans to secure his name in immortality and extricate himself from the humdrum parochialism of daily life, the circle of relationships which caused him anxiety, constrained and entrapped him. He was impatient to form associations with gifted men and ambitious youths. He formulated the project of *Hyperion*,[5] sketching out ideas which were later completely reshaped. The work, published in Schiller's *Die Horen* (*The Horae*), contained not a few lines which would find their way into the final work. It is clear to see how long he carried this piece within him, and perhaps here it is pertinent to remark that he did not work at speed and that whatever he conceived only came about through struggle. His thoughts were committed to paper more than once, undergoing repeated revisions and changes until such point as he felt their expression was at its purest and most consummate. This becomes evident on reading his papers, where we find the same poem a half-dozen times, passing through unceasing amendments.

His university comrades held him in high esteem and thought him extraordinary, though sometimes rather too tender and melancholic. On the whole, Hölderlin was not unsociable, though he did not join in with the wild cohort of students. I have been told that at this time he would sometimes retire for weeks on end and converse only with his mandolin, whose strains he accompanied in song. He lamented much and grievously, his sufferings exacerbated by a love too delicate and sentimental, by his zeal and impetuous cravings for fame and honour, the loathing of his circumstances, the aversion to his course of study. Surely this slough of miseries was enough to steer him towards complaint, without the fact that his fragile, easily piqued, childlike nature left him too rawly exposed to each impression and gave way too easily under the pressure of adversity. Gradually he became accustomed to a general dissatisfaction with human affairs as they stand today, and, by instead championing the cultural source, the ancient Greeks with their flourishing civilisation and virginal intellect eternally resplendent, developed an all too dangerous, unnatural contempt for the contemporary world.

This veneration of the Greeks led to a sense of discontentment with the land of his birth, made manifest through the attacks we find in *Hyperion* and which to my mind elicit a certain repugnance.

We observe, then, in this increasingly hostile reception to the world, which for him was nothing less than natural, the first indications of his state of despondency. Even at the moment of early blooming, before the real work had begun and in spite of the vision of a brighter future, these feelings still anchored themselves when there was nothing to sustain his imagination, his pride, his ambition, his world of dreams, but in circumstances which were hardly without happiness or could be termed insupportable. Had he been possessed of a sense of humour, a mind given to jokes and the gift of self-parody, had he understood something of men and the world, he might have summoned the reserves to stave off perdition. But his nature lacked this key element, his Muse knew only how to lament and weep, venerate and extol, but never indulge in mild tomfoolery or innocent play.

Yet no one then could have suspected that this magnificent youth would end up as an old man stricken by misery;

Friedrich von Matthisson[6] often said that he had never witnessed a more agreeable and engaging young man than was Hölderlin around this time.

How far his *Hyperion* had progressed while he remained at university I cannot say. The evidence shows that the idea, the plan and certain passages belong to this earlier period of his life. A good number of the lyric poems, which he later rejected, already reveal the full and beautifully pure heart we know from the more accomplished works; but these unique and deeply moving images, this virginal love inflamed by nature and sacred eternal joy already announce fatalistic notions and mournful anxieties due to that heightened, often overwrought faculty through which he sought expression, despite the fact that it was nature itself which he most worshipped and adored.

After completing his studies, he left Württemberg and became a tutor for a reputable Frankfurt family.[7] A young man who could assert himself in all manner of things, gifted with an indefatigable and questing spirit, an appealing physique, poet and musician, could surely not fail and must surely find happiness. The mother of his pupil, a young woman with a lively, enthusiastic and seemingly passionate soul, all too keenly sensed the bond of kinship the young man was experiencing and could not long hold out against Hölderlin's flute and mandolin, his piano-playing, his soft singing, his sensitivity, his refined and serene personality, his lovely glance, his youth, his eccentric spirit and distinguished gifts, aspects which combined to inflame the passions of this young woman, whose imagination was as fertile and highly strung as his own. Hölderlin loved immediately, powerfully and ardently, his whole heart plunged into the fire and was consumed. Even during the period of his madness twenty years on, letters were found in his possession from his beloved Diotima, letters which he had until then kept hidden. The young enthusiast stretched his forces of exaltation to breaking point, his days flowed by in this state of delirious love. He was suffused with the high-born ideas of Plato: he abandoned reality, languished in the delightful reverie of the present and laid the groundwork for a horrifying future.

This love liaison, pursued on both sides with equal passion, could not last and finally Hölderlin was obliged to leave the house in the most disagreeable manner, after the husband of his Diotima realised what was going on.[8] Hölderlin's pain was indescribable. The coddled youth, lulled by the sweet intoxication of this love entanglement, was suddenly pitched back into bitter reality. Admittedly it was not a total severance. The pair maintained a correspondence, agreed to meet in a single star which they would gaze at in the same moment, and they even managed to rendezvous at a property belonging to Diotima.[9] But Hölderlin now carried a fracture in his heart which, widening, became ever more dangerous, his soul was even more exalted than ever, his complaint more bitter and profligate, as now authentic reasons existed for the agony it expressed. Only the sating of his ambition, which was then at its climax, could have saved him.

He completed his *Hyperion*, a piece of writing on which I have nothing to add, since the reader can judge for himself. Allow me to recall though that in this work a terrible deadening pain suffuses everything and its entire poetic universe appears overhung by an oppressive nocturnal sky. On almost every page one encounters ideas which are virtual prophecies of their writer's own horrifying fate. All the flowers hang their heads. In spite of the sublime images of universal love and the fervent adoration of nature, of the primordial world and of Greece, the spirit of the novel, or rather suite of lyrical poems, is one of a grave incurable illness, which even from beauty extracts a morbid substance. It is an unnatural struggle against destiny, a wounded mawkishness, a black melancholy and an ill-fated perverseness through which the poet forcibly cleaves a path into madness.

Hölderlin travelled now to Weimar and then Jena, as so many other great men did. He burned with an ardour for glory, the craving to distinguish himself.[10] His most consummate poems date from this period. Such a rare talent, combined with the grace of his person, could not fail to make an impression. Now all was focused on the fulfilment of his ambition. Wounded as he was, bitter and on edge, he could not tolerate any obstacles placed in his path. It is said that his beloved Diotima came to his aid, forging liaisons with certain eminent men. The noble Schiller held him in great affection, respected his aspirations and declared that he possessed the most promising gift of all his countrymen. He tried to set him on the straight and narrow by helping to procure him a professorship. Had he assumed such a position, Hölderlin would have benefited from a clearly defined sphere of activity, he would have learned to set himself limits, his health would have improved, he would have regained strength, eased the load of his spiritual tension, he would have made himself useful and the presence of a woman at his side would have laid waste each of those unnatural directions which influenced his soul, instructed him how to guide his existence, how to live, work and effectively carry himself amongst humankind. But Hölderlin's unfortunate fate, coupled with the jealousy of his enemies, decided otherwise. Another got the post and he saw himself ultimately degraded. They say that Goethe was not good to him.

That appears to be true, for each time I mentioned Goethe in my conversations with him he denied any knowledge of the man, which for Hölderlin signified a hostile conviction. Schiller, on the other hand, and many others, he recalled often.[11] This, then, was the decisive blow against Hölderlin's spirit. He saw his best hopes dashed, his pride and his keen sense of himself besmirched, his talent and knowledge come to nothing, his aspirations judged unattainable, and he found himself once more watching the prospects of a happy future recede, like a pilgrim abandoned to an existence against whose harshness he had no remedy, an injustice his scant resources did not enable him to endure.

Then in the spring of 1791 he travelled to Switzerland where he met Lavater,[12] Zollikofer[13] and a few others, and there he composed powerful and beautiful songs and sketched out a tragedy. But the latter he was not in a position to complete. It is indisputable that his poetic talent lay in the lyric form rather than in the dramatic. He immersed himself in philosophy and Schelling's early works had a decisive effect on him, as he later recounted to me amidst a flood of incomprehensible words on Kant and Schelling. By then he had already fallen into a profound state of melancholy, which made him withdraw from the company of men, shut himself away in gloomy reverie and labour against every event to such an extent that ultimately he could no longer offer the least resistance to whatever else imposed itself on him. In this I mean the desperate efforts to forget everything through the intoxication of the senses, in disordered pleasures.

Something had to give. Hölderlin once again assumed the role of tutor in France. He was hardly cut out for a wild existence. He was born for a pure life, orderly, hardworking. He was aware that his physical constitution and spiritual nature could not be sustained if he was left insensible to such an extent that pleasure no longer related to feeling, in the same way that formerly he felt without it relating to any pleasure. It was not long before his spirit began to suffer due to such a disorientating way of life and he was given to outbursts of fury and rage.

For reasons which remain unexplained, he suddenly appeared again in his homeland, unnoticed, without a penny to his name and clothed in rags.[14] Herr von Matthisson told me that one day he was sat peacefully dining in his room when the door opened and a man entered whom he did not know. This figure was pale, cadaveric and scrawny, his eyes possessed a wild, vacant look, his hair and beard were long and he was dressed like a beggar. Terrified, Herr Matthisson stood up, staring fixedly at this frightful figure remained rooted there for quite some time without saying a word; then it advanced, leaned over the table, presented a hand with hideous long, untrimmed nails and murmured in a low, spectral voice: 'Hölderlin.' Right away the apparition withdrew, and the overwhelmed gentleman felt the urgent need to recover from the powerful impression made by this visit. Arriving at his mother's house in Nürtingen, Hölderlin chased her and the others gathered there from the house in a fit of rage.

He stayed with her for some time, and here knew moments of lucidity and well-being, though he was still assailed by bouts of the blackest melancholy. Again, but for the last time, his poor heart, so naked and defenceless, before love was enflamed. But he had to be parted from the object of his adoration and veneration; the girl ended up marrying a close relative of his. This was the last thread securing Hölderlin's tenuous grip on sanity. Despite her being close by, in his vicinity, Hölderlin refused to even acknowledge the woman again, claiming that he had never had the honour of meeting 'Her Majesty'.

At this time, a prince who had encountered Hölderlin in Jena heard of the poet's parlous state and had the notion to divert him from his trials by offering him an appropriate post and thus hopefully save him from mental collapse.[15] So he was appointed as the librarian. But Hölderlin was already lost. His outbursts of fury had become even more violent than before. He took on a translation of Sophocles, which proved a curious blend of the wondrous and the deranged.[16] Hölderlin could no longer be accommodated; under the pretext that he was to buy books in Tübingen, he was urged to travel there and on arrival was forcibly interned in a clinic where they sought to pursue a medical cure.

He remained there for two years,[17] but his lucid spirit was no more, his intellectual powers were depleted, his nerves hopelessly shattered, and so he sank into the deplorable state which he has known to this day. He was welcomed into the home of a carpenter,[18] where he has dwelled now for more than twenty years, occupying a small room with nothing more than a bed and a few rare books.

When you step today into the house of the unfortunate, you would not think you were to meet the poet who wandered willingly along the Ilisos with Plato; yet the place is not unpleasant: it is the house of a prosperous carpenter, a man who possesses an unusual culture for one of his position and who speaks readily of Kant, Fichte, Schelling, Novalis, Tieck and others. The visitor requests to be directed to the room of Herr Librarian – for this is how Hölderlin prefers to be addressed – and comes upon a little door. On the other side you can hear talking, and it seems there is quite a gathering. But the good carpenter confirms that he is quite alone and that he talks to himself day and night. You hesitate to knock, stricken with unease. Then you go ahead and do so, a forceful voice says, 'Come in!' You open the door; at the centre of the room stands a gaunt figure who, bowing deeply, affords you the greatest reverence, and does not cease to bestow on you compliments, making gestures which would be graceful if they were not so spasmodic. You admire the profile, the lofty brow heavy with thought, the affable, friendly eyes, their fire gone but not devoid of soul; you note the devastating traces of the malaise in the cheeks, the mouth, the nose and over the eyes, where a furrow runs painful and deep. Then you note with compassion and sorrow the convulsive movement which breaks out from time to time upon his face, which causes him to raise his shoulders and a trembling to course through his hands and fingers. He wears a simple doublet in the side pockets of which he likes to hide his hands. You manage a few words in an attempt to initiate a conversation, words which are welcomed with the most obliging of reverences and a torrent of senseless phrases which serve to discomfort the newcomer. As form dictates – and Hölderlin was always well mannered – that one address some courtesy to the guest, he feels obliged to say something friendly, to proffer a question. And this is what he does. You can make out a few comprehensible words, but most are so confused that it is impossible to offer a reply. In any case Hölderlin clearly anticipates no response and dispenses even greater linguistic confusion should the visitor attempt to pursue one of his ideas. We'll return to this later when exploring those conversations I had with him. Let us for now stick to the scene itself. The visitor now finds himself addressed as 'Your Majesty', 'Your Holiness' and 'Merciful Father'. But Hölderlin is extremely ill at ease: he receives such visits with great reluctance and always finds himself more tormented afterwards. It is for this reason that each time someone begged me to take them to see Hölderlin, I was loath to do so. Yet I still preferred being accompanied than visiting alone. For such an event was just too alarming, too distressing for the hermit, closed off as he was from all interaction with people, and the visitor did not know how to deal with it. Hölderlin soon began to express gratitude for the visit, bowing once more, and at this point it was wise to take one's leave.

People rarely spent much time with him. Even those from his past found such a meeting too bizarre, oppressive, wearing and in the end senseless. For even to them, Herr Librarian behaved in the most eccentric manner. Thus Friedrich Haug,[19] noted author of epigrams, whom he had known for years came to see him. He too was addressed as 'Your Majesty' and 'Baron von Haug'. However hard his friend tried to convince Hölderlin that he had not been ennobled, the poet refused to dispense with the title. For those visitors who were complete strangers to him, unbridled absurdity was a given. Here, then, I have tried to show how he appeared on the outside, but now let us examine further details.

At the beginning he wrote much and filled all the paper which was presented to him. These were letters in prose or in metred form, freely inspired by Pindar and addressed to his beloved Diotima, often odes in the alcaic style.[20] His writing exhibited a peculiar character, its content favoured the memory of times past, the struggle with God, the fêting of the Greeks. On the thought process which went into it we'll say nothing more for now.

In this early period with the carpenter he was still prone to fits of madness and rage, so much so that the carpenter had on occasion to subdue the raving poet with his own powerful fists. One time Hölderlin chased all the carpenter's apprentices out of the house and bolted the door on them. When he saw someone approaching from the clinic, he was subsumed by a paroxysm of fury and was riven with convulsions. Often when he walked freely out and about, he became the victim of mockery from those vile people who exist everywhere and whose bestiality is worse when they select for the object of their malice such an afflicted sacred spirit, a victim of pure misfortune. This made Hölderlin so embittered when he became aware of it that he threw mud and stones at his tormentors and his rage did not abate for another whole day. It is more dispiriting still to note that even some students have shown themselves sufficiently imbecilic by teasing him and provoking him into a rage. I shall say no more except that of all the mischief which is part and parcel of university life, this particular strain is surely the most inexcusable.

Regularly the carpenter's wife, or one of the daughters or sons, took the unfortunate out into the surrounding fields and vineyards. There he would sit on a stone patiently waiting for the return leg to the house. It is worth pointing out that they were obliged to act with him just as one does a small child, so as to reduce the chance of any disruptive behaviour. When he leaves the house, they have to remind him in advance to wash and groom himself, for his hands are habitually soiled from spending half the day tearing up grass. Once dressed, he hangs back, refusing to take the lead. When he passes a two-year-old child and he is not too distracted, he will raise his hat, which he tends to wear low over his brow. It is worth mentioning too the laudable truth that the townspeople who knew him never mocked him, but let him go on his way unmolested, though they spoke amongst themselves, 'Ah . . . how intelligent and perceptive was this man once and now look at him, he is completely insane.' But really the carpenter's family did not like him going out alone, they would rather he remained in the enclosure before the house.

At first he paid regular visits to the eminent Conz,[21] who has just departed us. This diligent and hard-working friend of ancient literature owned a garden in Tübingen near the Hirschauer Gate to which, an hour before noon, his daily walk would take him, in virtue of a habit cultivated over many decades. For a quarter of a century you would see his heavy frame pass along and then stop immediately in front of the gate, where the gatekeeper would carefully light his pipe for him. After this the poet would continue slowly and peacefully on his way and linger for a few hours outside in the open air or in the summer house. When Conz was working on his translation of Aeschylus, Hölderlin, who back then still possessed fire and strength, would go to see him there. He amused himself by picking garden flowers, and when he had gathered a nice bouquet he tucked it into his pocket. Sometimes Conz gave him a book. Once he reported to me that Hölderlin leaned over his bed and began to read some verses of the Aeschylus text. But right afterwards he began to cry out with a crampy laugh, 'I don't understand any of this! It's all in the Kalamatta tongue.'[22] For amongst Hölderlin's eccentricities, there was also the invention of new words.

As he weakened and grew more vague, his visits to Conz tailed off. From time to time I had to incite him to walk with me to the gardens of Conz. He poured forth all sorts of objections, saying, 'I don't have time, Your Holiness!', for I too received various titles, 'I am waiting on a visit', or else he employed the strange formal statement he was wont to use: 'They order me to remain here.' On occasion, when the weather was bright and clear, I urged him to dress and we would set out. Once, it was a day in spring, he was delighted by the flowering shrubs and the profusion of blooms. He extolled the beauty of the garden in the most charming manner. But apart from this isolated case he was always irrational when he was alone with me. Conz tried to encourage him to remember earlier days, but all in vain. One time he said: 'The Counsellor Haug, whom you

45

remember well, has recently made a very beautiful poem.'
Hölderlin, who was habitually inattentive to what people
said to him, declared: 'Has he made one?' Conz laughed
heartily at this. We returned to the house and in the street
Hölderlin, at the moment of farewell, kissed the hand of
Herr Conz in the most elegant manner.

His day is extremely simple. In the morning, particularly
in summer, when he is without a doubt more agitated
and troubled, he rises before or with the sun and leaves
the house to go and walk within the enclosure. This walk
lasts for around four to five hours, until such point as he
returns exhausted. He entertains himself by taking out a
handkerchief which he keeps in his pocket and flapping it
against the fence posts or else tearing up clumps of grass.
Whatever he finds he pockets, whether it be a piece of iron
or a scrap of leather. Furthermore, he talks incessantly
to himself, questioning and responding, sometimes yes
sometimes no, and often both at the same time. For he
loves to respond in the negative.

Thereupon he enters the house and wanders about.
They bring him his meals in his room and he eats heartily,
relishing also the wine which they serve him, of which he
would drink as much as he could. When he has finished
he can no longer bear the sight of the dirty crockery and

so right away places it on the floor at the threshold of the room. He wants nothing in that room but what belongs to him, everything else is placed in front of the door. The remainder of the day is whiled away in monologues and pacing back and forth in the little chamber.

What can occupy him for a whole day is his *Hyperion*. Hundreds of times, when I paid him a visit, I heard him declaiming from it in a loud voice. His pathos was impressive and *Hyperion* almost always was there lying at hand. Often he would read me passages. When he had finished a particular part, he would exclaim with ponderous gesticulations: 'Wonderful, wonderful, Your Majesty!' He began reading again and then suddenly sat down, saying: 'You see gracious sir, a comma!' He also read aloud the books I had offered to him. But he understood nothing of them because he was too distracted, he could never even follow one of his own thoughts, still less that of someone else. Yet he praised the book to the hilt, employing all his customary sagacity.

The only other books are the *Odes* of Klopstock,[23] those of Gleim,[24] Cronegk[25] and other older poets of this stable. He reads often the *Odes* and often quotes from them.

I told him innumerable times that his *Hyperion* would be reprinted and that Uhland and Schwab were in the midst of collating his poems. But I received no response other than a deep bow and the words: 'You are a good soul, Herr Waiblinger! I am obliged to you, Your Holiness.' Often when he cut off proceedings in this way, I wanted to wrest from him some statement that made sense. I rejigged my phrasing, pushed on, pressing the same idea in a slightly different way and only gave in when Hölderlin's movements became more violent and a stream of deranged words began to flow from his lips.

The carpenter soon became surprised at the power I could wield over him, persuading him to accompany me whenever I wished, and that he was even preoccupied with me in my absence. What pleased him most about me was the summer house I resided in on the Österberg,[26] the place where Wieland committed to paper the first blooms of his Muse. From there you looked down over the friendly green vales, over the city with its towering castle hill, over the bend of the Neckar, over countless laughing villages and the Alpine range. It is now more than five years since I passed a carefree summer there, amidst that verdure, before that inspiring view, in the open air. Unfortunately such an oppressive burden weighed on my spirit at that time that even the joy of this bucolic nature could not bring me cheer or stiffen my inward resolve. I wrote a novel there which I soon realised should be cast into the fire, for there was little in it that did not cause me to be rightly ashamed. But it was in this place that the song of Kalonasora was conceived, which when it was published three years later at least brought plaudits to the author from critics and the friends of poetry. It was to this place, then, that once a week I would escort Hölderlin. On reaching the garden house and entering, Hölderlin would bow and praise my grace and generosity. He would draw on all kinds of formal politesse, and it often seemed as if by doing this he wished to deliberately keep everyone at arm's length. That there was something behind the habit seems certain, but it would be folly to insist that every gesture and action on Hölderlin's part had some logical explanation, beyond straightforward idiosyncrasy or eccentricity.

Hölderlin opened the window, sat before it and began to wax lyrical on the view in the most lucid terms. I noticed that he was generally in a better state when in the open air. He spoke to himself less, which for me proved that he was becoming more clear-headed: in fact I was convinced that this unceasing monologue with himself was nothing more than the disequilibrium of thought and his inability to gain significant purchase on any object. I'll return to this later. I kept Hölderlin well supplied with snuff and pipe tobacco, both of which gave him immense pleasure. With a pinch of snuff I could lift his heart, and when I filled his pipe and lit it for him, he would praise both tobacco and pipe in the most impassioned terms; for him this was the nearest thing to unalloyed contentment. He had ceased talking, and because he was happy and to disturb him now would be imprudent, I let him be while I indulged in some reading of my own.

He held a particular fascination for the pantheistic *One and All* inscribed in giant Greek letters on the wall above my work desk. Often he conversed at length with himself while observing this mysterious inscription so ponderous with thought, and once he declared: 'From this day on I am orthodox, Your Holiness! No, no, I am presently studying three volumes by Herr Kant and I am most interested in the new philosophy.' I asked him if he remembered Schelling. 'Yes of course, he studied at the same time as me, Herr Baron!' I informed Hölderlin that he was now living at Erlangen and he said: 'Formerly he lived in Munich.' He asked if I had ever spoken to him and I replied in the affirmative.

And that particular event occurred amidst the most mysterious set of circumstances in the world. In Stuttgart I had hoped to make Schelling's acquaintance, but I only learned of his presence when he was on the point of leaving, and Counsillor Haug, who wanted to introduce me to him, passed on a few flattering words about me that he had left in his wake. When later I visited Erlangen, I was keen to see Schelling. Arriving at his residence, I found no one who could formally announce my presence. A deathly silence reigned. I had no idea which floor or door to approach, so I remained in a hallway; such an unearthly wait just made me laugh. No, I thought, I shall not depart the house of the great philosopher until I have made his acquaintance; surely some sign of life must make

50

itself known in this house, where all that is on earth and in heaven finds its rightful place. Suddenly I heard someone coughing. Schelling! I said to myself: it was him, it had to be. Boldly and without further ado I advanced to the door from behind which the sound came. I knocked. Almost at the same instant, a man whose physiognomy answered to that of a philosopher stood in the doorway. Drily Schelling asked me if I was known to the house, and enquired if I would care to meet him after he had finished his repast, which he was then about to take. Calmly I contemplated his face, but I abruptly took my leave and departed. So then, I told myself, now you have seen Schelling and you have even spoken with him, but clearly at the most inopportune moment! I never even told him my name. I have no idea what absurd caprice caused me not to renew my visit, to just leave immediately, satisfied with having spoken to the philosopher at the moment when perhaps he was still burning in the ardour of his *Ages of the World*.[27]

Permit me to return to Hölderlin. He remembered Matthisson, Schiller, Zollikofer, Lavater, Heinse[28] and many others, but, as I already noted, never Goethe. His memory at least demonstrated an element of power and endurance. I found it odd that he had hung on the wall a portrait of Frederick the Great and I asked him why. He merely replied: 'You already pointed this out before, Herr Baron.' And yes I do remember making this same remark some months before. He also recognised all those whom he had already met. He never forgot that I was a poet and enquired innumerable times what I was working on and if I was truly dedicated to my craft. But then right after this he might say: 'I for one, kind sir, no longer have the same name. From now on I am to be known as Killalusimeno. Yes Your Majesty: You asserted as much. It's of no consequence to me!'

This last I heard from him often. It was if he sought to restore his equilibrium and bring calm by offering this 'It's of no consequence to me.'

I gave him paper to write on. Then he would sit at his desk and produce a few lines, metrically rhymed. Admittedly they were senseless, particularly the last ones, but at least they were consistent in their rhyming form. He would rise and hand me his work with the most effusive compliments. Once he wrote at the base of the page: 'Your most humble Hölderlin.'

One time I informed him there would be a concert that evening. I had mused whether this might be a pleasurable diversion for him. But it would have been folly to let him go alone. Perhaps the music would have made too great an impression on him, or the rowdiness of the students might have made him take fright. So we took our leave from the garden house. He was completely withdrawn into himself and not a word issued from his lips. But once we were in town, he looked upon me as if he were waking from sleep and stated: 'Concert.' He had certainly been mulling it over in the meantime.

For music had not entirely deserted him. He still played the piano correctly, albeit in a most eccentric style. When he sits at the keyboard, he remains there for days on end. He begins to labour over a theme of childish simplicity, and plays it over several hundred times in such a way that one can bear it no longer. Furthermore, a wave of spasms takes hold of him, causing his hands to race across the keyboard with dazzling speed, to the unpleasant clattering sound of his long fingernails. He refuses to have these trimmed and various ploys are required to induce him to do so, as one might for a stubborn child. After he has played for a certain time and his spirit has mellowed, he lowers his eyes, then lifts his head and, with a languishing, fading air, starts to sing. But in what language? That I could never discern, however many times I heard him, but he performed with profound pathos and it caused a shiver to pass along every nerve to hear him sing in this manner. Melancholy and sorrow formed the soul of his song: one could tell that he had once been a fine tenor.

Children he loves very much. But they take fright before him and run away. He is in dread of death and generally exists in a heightened state of anxiety. The extreme delicacy of his nerves makes him easily alarmed. He starts at the slightest sound. When he is agitated, angry or just of bilious temper, his whole face quivers, his gestures seem sharp, he twists his fingers into such knots you would think there were no joints, and he shrieks loudly, or blusters in raging discourses addressed to himself. In such moments it is wise to leave him alone until he has recovered from his seething, otherwise he will lead you briskly outside by the arm. If he suffers a particularly severe fury, he takes to his bed and remains there for several days.

One day, quite suddenly, the notion seized him that he would journey to Frankfurt. They then removed his boots, which so enraged the Herr Librarian that he stayed in bed for five whole days. But in summer anxieties plague him so often that entire nights are spent endlessly pacing the house.

I wanted to procure other books for him and thought that he would read Homer, whose name still lay lodged somewhere in his memory. I brought him a translation but he would not accept it. I gave it to the carpenter and told him to say that it belonged to him. But still Hölderlin would not accept it. The reason is not pride, but fear of being made unduly anxious by reading something unknown to him. Only what was familiar could bring him peace, *Hyperion* and his dusty old poets: for twenty years Homer had been a stranger to him and any novelty was an intrusion.

I invited him to accompany me to a garden where there was a wine tavern. The view here was very attractive and one could relax unobserved. Hölderlin imbibed with virility. Even the beer pleased him. He held it far better than you might think. However, I ensured proper limits were always respected. In such a place he felt entirely at ease when he smoked his pipe. He no longer spoke and his behaviour took on a restful quality.

He wrote to his aged mother, but always had to be urged to do so. These letters were not irrational; he took trouble over them and they were even lucid. But their style was that of a child who cannot write in a fully developed way or sustain a thought. In fact, one of them was quite good, but then it ended, 'I see now that I must come to a close.' At this point he had become disorientated, was aware of his confusion and thus ground to a halt. One might compare this state of disturbed thought to that experienced in illnesses, migraines, extreme drowsiness, or the morning hangover caused by an evening of intemperate consumption of wine. My garden house became so dear to him that he still enquired of it years after I had moved from there, and when he went with the carpenter's wife for a walk through a vineyard close by, he several times climbed to the door of the little house and firmly insisted that Herr Waiblinger lived there.

Nature, a good walk, the open sky always did him good. He is fortunate in the cheerful prospect offered by the little room over the Neckar, which bathes the feet of his house, to savour a charming patch of meadow and mountain scenery. Clear and luminous images taken from this view thus pass into his poetry, which he sets down on paper when the carpenter provides him with some.

It is remarkable that he is unwilling to speak about subjects which in his former days dominated his spirit. Of Frankfurt, Diotima, Greece, his poetry and other such things which were important to him he remains silent, and if you were to say, 'It is some time since you have set foot in Frankfurt', he would reply with a bow: 'Oui, Monsieur,[29] in your opinion.' Whereupon a flood of the most eccentric French issues forth.

It gave him immense pleasure when in recent years they installed a sofa in his little room. He reported this to me with childish delight when I came to visit. Having kissed my hand, he said: 'Observe kind sir, I now have a sofa.' I had to take a seat without delay, and for a long while afterwards Hölderlin would be sat on this sofa when I saw him.

At the time of my visits to him I made a number of excursions to Italy, Switzerland and the Tyrol, and on my return he always recalled where I had been and said he was particularly fond of Switzerland, especially the beautiful region around Zurich and St Gallen, and spoke of Lavater and Zollikofer. Once I told him I was travelling to Rome and would not be back for some time, jokingly suggesting he accompany me. He smiled as graciously and knowingly as only a sage can, and said: 'I must stay at home, I cannot go travelling any more, kind sir.'

Sometimes he gave answers which in all honesty made you laugh, especially when he delivered them with the face of one who was in fact scoffing. I once asked him how old he now was and he replied: 'Seventeen, Herr Baron.' But no irony is here intended; rather it is proof of the complete scattering of his mind. He never grasps what is said to him, because he is locked in a perpetual struggle with obscure and fleeting thoughts. When someone wants to wrest him from his gloomy ponderings with a question, they must be prepared to accept whatever comes first to his lips. Once I strolled with him across a meadow; I left him alone to walk beside me sunk deep inside himself. Then, drawing his attention to a newly built edifice, I said: 'Look, Herr Librarian, I am certain you have not noticed this building before.' Hölderlin roused himself and uttered in a tone which seemed to suggest the whole world depended on the answer: 'Oui, Your Majesty.'

I have safeguarded in Germany a collection of his writings and many other penned remnants of his melancholy existence and I would gladly share them were I able to. I recall only an ode, written in alcaic metre, which opens with the following lovely lines:

> To Diotima
> *If out of the distance that separates us,*
> *I am still recognisable to you, past,*
> *Oh you companion of my torments,*
> *Some good might still betoken you.*

In the final line you can see how he struggles to sustain an idea; he begins to come across like a fledgling bard or a poetaster who cannot find the means to clarify his poetic statement, devoid of the mastery to select phrases which properly express the strength of his feeling.

In his letters there is the recurrent theme of struggle and conflict with deity and fate, as he prefers to call them. So he writes: 'Celestial deity, how it has been for us, when I have come through various battles and won several notable victories.'

I once discovered amongst his papers a terrifying phrase replete with mystery. After honouring the renown of a list of Greek heroes and the beauty of the realm of gods, he says: 'Now for the first time I understand humankind, because I dwell far from it and in solitude.'

The appreciation of nature remained unsullied in him. It is an impressive and most edifying thought that the sanctified all-loving Mother Nature that Hölderlin celebrated in his most hale, most powerful and freshest verse still offered him in his darkest hours a thread to follow, something that remained eminently comprehensible after his once-clear spirit had plunged into the most atrocious confusion. The evidence is in his comportment in the open air, the calming, restorative effect that being outside seems to have, and especially the countless sublime images he draws from nature as he gazes from his open window, watching spring come and go. In verse vividly displaying

Homeric wisdom, he depicts how sheep wander over a path. That was something he often saw from his window. In another example he verged on a sublime thought as he watched the silver raindrops fall from his eaves.

But in vain does he seek any sense of cohesive articulation, for whenever he attempts to give expression to the abstract, he becomes confused, thwarted, and must in the end resort to his word choice being left to providence.

The greatest error into which numerous cursory critics of Hölderlin's confused mental state fall is to imagine that he was somehow fixed on the idea of only associating with kings, popes and persons of nobility, because he accords everyone such titles, even the carpenter. But this is completely untrue. In Hölderlin no single fixed idea predominates. His state is one of weakness rather than insanity, and all the expressions he gives of unreason are the direct consequence of this physical and mental atrophy. Let us try to explain this more clearly.

Hölderlin became incapable of holding a thought, of giving it clarity, of following it and linking it to another by way of analogy and thus to articulate a distant idea in a regular consistent sequence. His existence, as we have seen, consists of unswerving inwardness and this has to be one of the chief reasons why he sank into this deadened, restricted state of being from which ultimately he cannot extricate himself, a state exacerbated by his physical softening and the inordinate feebleness of his nerves. When something comes to his mind, a memory or perhaps a remark, roused by some object from the exterior world, he begins to think. But he lacks the calm, the mental solidity and the resolve to grasp what emerges to him through a fog. He ought to develop an idea, but again he has been relieved of the power to analyse any one concept. He wishes to affirm something, but since reality – being the end product of a healthy and organised mind – does not concern him, he refutes it at the same moment, for his spirit is a realm which sustains only fog and what is feigned. When for example he says to himself: 'Men are happy', he lacks the grounded-ness and lucidity to ask why and how this might be so; he experiences a dull, reticent feeling, so retracts his statement and says: 'Men are unhappy' without bothering to concern himself over the reasons why. Countless times I have noted this unfortunate contrariness, which consumes his thought even at the moment of its conception, since he customarily thinks out loud. As soon as he managed to hold a thought for some distance, it turned his head, confusion redoubled, his brow was overcome with terrible nervous convulsions, he shook his head and would cry out, 'No, no!' And to get clear of the dizziness caused by chronic anxiety, he would a few moments later let himself sink into the comforting balm of madness, firing out words without meaning or any signification, as if his spirit, in a sense overstretched by such a drawn-out thought, could restore itself only by having his mouth issue words which bore no relation to any of it. This becomes all too clear on reading through his papers. He tends to add a phrase which doubtless corresponds vaguely to the theme he wishes to develop. This phrase is clear and right, though it is more often than not a memory. But as soon as he begins to give it form, to elaborate, to engineer something, when he tries to mine the seam of the memories which remain to him and to give birth to some new thought, he loses purchase. Instead of a *single* thread connecting all his diverse thoughts, there exists a woven tangle of comings and goings, like a spider's web. Right after the birth he is languid, passing from one thought to the other, and finally utters his words or attempts to write with the same laboriousness, producing thoughts and the written word more akin to those of an untrained child when trying to express itself in writing. His head is still brimming with a host of sublime metaphysical notions, indeed even original poetic expressions, but can only communicate them in the most obscure and fantastical manner. He lacks the capacity to retain his vaporous imaginings, or approach such memories with a new angle of vision, with clear consistency, yet he is at pains to hide his confusion deliberately behind a form and manner of speaking over which he at least still commands some power.

To this category belong those pieces which appear in the anthology of his poems. Though they may contain something beautiful, fresh, lucid, and have passages which are wonderfully spirited, you observe here and there shoals, like shadow spots on the surface of clear, sunny water. Here Hölderlin's spirit, whose suffering begins at the very moment these poems I speak of were written down, is already submerged and thus he is no longer able to properly exploit the material. It might have been a wise thing if the editors Uhland and Schwab, who made their selections with such scrupulous attention and care, had left these poems out of proceedings, or included a note for those not up to speed with Hölderlin's acute nervous state. The sensitive editors displayed exemplary virtue in their regard for a poet still living, who in any case showed not the slightest interest in the publication of his poems.

Likewise, he is constantly preoccupied with himself, when he is not plunged into a state of mental torpor. When now he encounters another person, the most varied themes emerge and make him resolutely incomprehensible and impenetrable. In the first instance he is habitually thrown back in on himself and is oblivious to all that occurs on the outside. There exists between himself and the rest of humanity an immeasurable chasm. He has resolved to depart from mankind in the same way his own powers have departed him. No link between the two can now be discerned, unless they be put down to mere memory, habit, to need and instinct, which cannot be entirely subjugated. One day, for example, he was stricken with extreme fear to see a child perched on a window in a potentially dangerous position and he rushed forward to help. But this apparently humane action was really only a posthumous trace of his soul, formerly so deeply sensitive, open and warm-hearted. This was nothing more than the functioning of an instinctual drive. If you told him that the Greeks had been exterminated down to the last man, or that they now exist in an independent state, he would be indifferent; he would not even have retained the information or reflected upon it, for that is all too far away and too troubling to entertain. If you told him I had died, he would say with great fervour: 'Lord Jesus, is he dead?' But in the moment he would not have thought anything, not experienced anything. These words, so precisely communicative, would for him have been only pure forms which he might later reflect on; gradually they would penetrate and he would perhaps speak of my demise. Beyond that there would be very little: for he can simply no longer tolerate others.

This perpetual distraction, this over-concern for himself, this complete lack of participation in and interest for any events outside himself, this aversion and incapacity to wish to grasp, recognise, understand, to allow in another individuality other than his own – all these reasons mean that any rational communication with him is impossible.

Furthermore, let us not forget that a powerful vanity, a sort of pride inhabits him. All this was nourished by twenty years of solitude: because he lived totally cut off from the world, he became used to no longer needing it; and because no possibility was offered him to forge any joyful contact with the world, he consoled and anaesthetised himself with grandiose, proud illusions and from then on maintained an exalted existence entirely closed in on itself, reflecting back that former world in which he was accorded some measure of fame. Now he is I and not-I, world and man, first and second person, high or highest. But this grand opinion he has of himself is concealed behind the amiable grace and undeniable generosity of his nature, his breeding, innate and natural decency, a sense of propriety – values which his current spiritual degradation and confusion interfere with only fleetingly. Due to his association with eminent men of all kinds, even people of high rank, this high self-regard never surfaced, and Hölderlin carried himself with a modesty which captured the hearts of many. All these forms of courtesy and amicability are so ingrained in him that he reverts to them in his relations with everyone. But due to the lengthy nature of his seclusion and the acuteness of his mental decline, he has indulged in the most outrageous absurdities, exaggerating every formality and ceremonial greeting, addressing people as Majesty, Holiness, Baron and Father. It should not be overlooked that he was at court when madness decisively overcame him and that pride, vanity and the craving to be someone of note and influence are all factors in his now keeping everyone at an insurmountable distance. The idea that he truly believes he is in the company of kings should not be given credence; for, as I emphasised before, he is not a madman per se, has no fixed, deranged ideas, his state is merely one of spiritual exhaustion, a sickness which has become incurable due to the disordered nature of his nervous system.

Because he avoids anything that causes him disturbance and mental stress, he only manages to recall the fundamental developments of his earlier life which brought about his malady. But when he ponders them, he becomes distinctly ill at ease, raves, cries aloud, roams around the whole night long, unable to relax until his massively overstrained physical self reassumes its right to self-preservation. When he becomes enraged or irritable, as when he got it into his head to suddenly travel to France, he bitterly retreats to his little room, within whose confines he has reduced the whole world, and there he reduces himself even further, so as to remain secure and at peace so he can better manage the suffering. Then he lies down on his bed.

The surplus of absurdities that he addresses to himself and to others is the consequence of his penchant for conversing alone. He is a solitary, he becomes bored, he needs to speak to himself. He says something reasonable, but he cannot follow it any further or lead it anywhere, something outside of himself enters his head, is supplanted and destroyed by a second thought and then a third, a fourth. What results is a diabolical confusion, he is now talking gibberish. Meaningless words issue forth while his spirit tries to regain some measure of balance. If he is in the company of others, he feels he should be courteous, gregarious, enquire something of someone without really caring what the answer might be. In such situations he becomes so filled with tension that he no longer sees the person he has addressed and resorts to talking to himself. If he finds himself in a position of having to provide a response he cannot come up with anything, nor does he even properly grasp what has been said to him, because his attention span is non-existent and so he treats the interlocutor to more extravagant balderdash.

His legion of nonsensical eccentricities are mostly the result of his life in seclusion. If the so-called rational people develop odd habits when they withdraw for many years from the exterior world, especially when they have stopped working, then imagine what it's like for an unfortunate who in his youth was regaled with hope, joys, beauty and riches and now must live cut off from society for decades due to an unhappy circumstance of simply possessing an over-sensitised spiritual nature, a too highly strung soul, reduced to killing time by tinkering with the disorganised mechanism of its faculty of thought.

If I had to now reply to the question which irresistibly poses itself to us when we consider the moving destiny of this once so promising spirit, if he could somehow recover his faculties, reawaken and rediscover the sum of his intellectual powers, I must confess with the most profound sense of pain that such a transformation, however desirable, is not likely to happen. Hölderlin's corporeal make-up is so constructed that to free his spirit from this alienation he would have to acquire a fresh set of nerves. Yet still we can hope and believe, with a view to a number of other experiences, in a momentary restoration, which the unfortunate might experience before the final severing of the bond which for him has been the cause of such suffering, that between the soul and the body. But this would only be for a moment, and the final occasion. When I left Germany, Hölderlin had already declined significantly, he was more depleted than formerly and seemed calmer. Six years ago his glance still betrayed fire and strength, his face showed vitality and warmth. But later he had taken on a wearier aspect, seemed more worn out, faded. It has been a long time since I have had news of him. He has now borne his existence for fifty-seven years, of which only the first thirty really count. No other soul is more worthy than his to find liberation from a body that holds back its inner life, its most sublime powers, its most audacious flight, a soul whose make-up is too tense, strained and vulnerable, a soul which the storms of fate have torn asunder! Let us hope, then, that one final episode of lucidity will be afforded this noble being, this friend cut off from our community, and before his passage into another life the melancholic enigma of the past will become that much clearer and hope for the future will be newly revived!

Transcribed in the winter of 1827–8

Endnotes

1. *Ludwig Uhland* (1787–1862) – German philologist and lyric poet of the Romantic school who was born and died in Tübingen, best known as author of his work from 1809, 'Der gute Kamerad' ('The Good Comrade'), a patriotic ballad dear to the German armed forces and almost a national hymn.

2. *Gustav Schwab* (1792–1850) – German pastor, publisher and writer who was born and died in Stuttgart. A close friend of Uhland, he studied at Tübingen and later worked there as a pastor. In 1813, on a trip to northern Germany, he met Goethe, Schleiermacher, Rückert, von Chamisso and other literary notables.

3. The 'Tübinger Stift' was founded as an Augustinian monastery in the Middle Ages, and today still serves as a centre of board and lodging, a hall of residence for students with a scholarship. Hölderlin was one of the famous 'Stiftler', along with Hegel and later Schelling. Waiblinger himself was a student there from 1822 to 1826.

4. In 1786 Hölderlin, at the age of sixteen, entered the Monastery of Maulbronn and there fell in love with the administrator's youngest daughter, Luise Nast. They were engaged in 1788, but Hölderlin broke it off the following year, after his admission to the

Tübingen seminary. In a letter to her dated 1790, he put this sudden U-turn down to an 'insurmountable melancholy' caused by thwarted ambition.

5. *Hyperion* is Hölderlin's key work aside from his poems, an epistolary novel in two volumes, published successively in 1797 and 1799. It constitutes a series of letters written to one Bellarmin and further letters to Hyperion's love Diotima. The work is set in Greece and unfolds within the scenario of youthful Greeks fighting for independence. Hölderlin presented the first version of *Hyperion* to Schiller in 1794 and a fragment was published in the review *Thalia*. In 1797 the whole of the first volume then appeared in *Die Horen* (*The Horae*), a monthly literary journal edited by Schiller. The second part appeared there in 1799.

6. *Friedrich von Matthisson* (1761–1831) – German poet best known for his poem 'Adelaide', which was set to music by Beethoven and hence made famous. Matthisson was lauded by Schiller, and Hölderlin encountered him at the Tübingen seminary.

7. In August 1795, Hölderlin was offered a post in Frankfurt as tutor to the children of the respectable Gontard family. He took up his post the following January. There he entered into a perilous liaison with Susette Gontard (Diotima).

8. On 25 September 1798 Hölderlin abruptly left Frankfurt after an embarrassing altercation with the

husband of his lover. It is widely believed that the trauma of this severance contributed crucially to Hölderlin's descent into the shadows.

9. In the immediate aftermath of the termination of the liaison Hölderlin found sanctuary with a friend, Isaac von Sinclair, who counselled him and took him to the court of Homburg, where he found employment as court librarian. On 6 February 1800 Hölderlin met Susette Gontard in secret, and then on 8 May they saw each other for the last time. Hölderlin continued to work as a tutor in France and Switzerland. On 30 June 1802, it was Sinclair who gave Hölderlin the news that his Diotima had died from influenza.

10. Waiblinger appears confused here with his timeline. In fact, Hölderlin left for Jena in 1795; there he enrolled at the university, attended classes by Fichte and even met Novalis.

11. In spite of Schiller's enthusings, Goethe appeared to have overlooked Hölderlin's genius and showed little interest in his work. This peculiar snub by the greatest man of the age in German letters played into the mix of Hölderlin's sense of being apart and misunderstood, rejected by his era.

12. Johann Kaspar Lavater (1741–1801) – Swiss poet, philosopher, theologian and most importantly physiognomist, whose works were greatly admired by Goethe.

13. Georg Joachim Zollikofer (1730–88) – Swiss German theologian who popularised 'Enlightenment' theology. Renowned for his preaching and sermons on this subject.

14. On 10 December 1801, Hölderlin left Nürtingen and his mother's house on foot to travel to Bordeaux to take up a teaching post. On the 15th he was arrested and detained by the French army in Strasbourg. Released on the 30th, he reached Lyon on 8 January 1802, and finally Bordeaux on the 28th. But halfway through May he suddenly abandoned his post and walked all the way back to Germany.

15. Friedrich von Hessen-Homburg, in whose service was Isaac Sinclair.

16. Hölderlin and Sinclair visited Schelling in June 1804 and took him a copy of Hölderlin's new eccentrically designed translation of Sophocles. On 14 July Schelling wrote in a letter to Hegel: 'His translation of Sophocles already belies the decline of his mind.'

17. Hölderlin was forcibly detained at the clinic of Autenrieth, Tübingen. He left in early May 1807.

18. Ernst Zimmer and his family took in Hölderlin after his release from the clinic due to his own family's indifference. Zimmer, a cultured man, had visited Hölderlin at the clinic and been shocked to see the woeful state befallen such a talented and noble-minded man. The clinic suggested Zimmer take Hölderlin to

his home by the Neckar and all agreed it would be the ideal environment for him.

19. Friedrich Haug (1761–1829) – German poet, notable for his two volumes of epigrams which appeared in 1802.

20. In the style of the archaic Greek poet, a contemporary of Sappho.

21. Carl Philipp Conz (1762–1827) – German poet and professor of Greek and Roman literature at Tübingen. Hölderlin met him at the seminary.

22. Hölderlin presumably refers to the language spoken at Kalamata in the Peloponnese, which is mentioned in Homer's *The Iliad*.

23. Friedrich Gottlieb Klopstock (1724–1803) – German poet and dramatist best known for his epic poem *Der Messias* (*The Messiah*). His 'Odes', which so obsessed Hölderlin according to Waiblinger, take the form of hymns and demonstrate religious and mythological themes, thereby echoing or influencing in some measure Hölderlin's own style.

24. Johann Wilhelm Ludwig Gleim (1719–1803) – German poet and literary patron.

25. Johann Friedrich von Cronegk (1731–58) – German poet.

26. A hill situated to the east of Tübingen. Here Wieland wrote his *Oberon*. He invited poets like Waiblinger and Mörike to visit his summer house and savour the romantic idyll.

27. The *Weltalter*, Schelling's major philosophical work of 1811.
28. Wilhelm Heinse (1746–1803) – German writer.
29. In French in the original German text.

Wilhelm Waiblinger
(1804–30)

A poet of the so-called second generation of German Romantics and a friend of the better-known Eduard Mörike, Waiblinger is best remembered today for his association with Friedrich Hölderlin. During the 1820s Waiblinger and Mörike were members of the same seminary in Tübingen which Hölderlin had attended decades earlier. In his short story *In Pressel's Garden House* (1913) Hermann Hesse memorably paints a visit made by the two young theology students to Hölderlin. Learning of the legendary figure dwelling in the tower on the Neckar riverfront, the ardent Waiblinger sought to gain access and meet the reputedly difficult and solitary great poet. Unlike most newcomers, Waiblinger was curiously tolerated, so began from the summer of 1822 a series of visits and ultimately a burgeoning friendship which led to the writing of Waiblinger's later memoir of Hölderlin. Like his more famous English brethren, Waiblinger was drawn to the South, to Italy, and arrived there in 1826. Steeped in the works of Dante, he sought to emulate his master. Whilst there he found time to write *Friedrich Hölderlin's Life, Poetry and Madness* from memory. Following Waiblinger's premature death it was published in 1831 and included in the first edition of Hölderlin's *Collected Works* (1839–46).

Friedrich Hölderlin
(1770–1843)

Johann Christian Friedrich Hölderlin was born in Lauffen am Neckar in Württemberg, the same river beside which he died seventy-three years later. A series of family bereavements marked his early life; he lost his father at the age of two and was brought up by his mother. Hölderlin saw his childhood as one experienced in an 'orphan-state', saturated by grief, loss and sorrow. In 1786 as a student at the Maulbronn Monastery Hölderlin had fallen in love with the administrator's daughter, Luise Nast, the first of such inwardly turbulent doomed affairs.

In 1788, his spirit soaring with the odes of Klopstock and Pindar, Hölderlin moved to Tübingen where he attended the 'Stift', or seminary, and studied Lutheran theology in the illustrious company of the future philosophers Hegel and Schelling. Following this period Hölderlin experienced an interweaving of poetic and philosophical activity before concentrating on poetry as the purest form in which to access truth. He began to write *Hyperion*, an epistolary novel, a collection of letters between a modern Greek hero and his German friend, the first volume of which appeared in 1797. *Hyperion*, whose first instalment was published in Schiller's review *Thalia*, sought to provide insight into the struggle between a lost state of harmony, of unity symbolised by Hellenism and the over-riding propulsion of the human spirit towards freedom. A move to Jena in 1794 saw Hölderlin's poetic thought develop further, encouraged to greater heights by the fervent intellectual climate of that city and meetings with Fichte and Novalis. Whilst in Jena Hölderlin found work as a private tutor and fell deeply in love with his pupil's mother, Susette Gontard, who became Diotima in *Hyperion*. The inevitable failure of the affair and consequent fallout had a disastrous and corrosive effect on Hölderlin's state of mental health. Dispirited by the trials of love and finding philosophy a frustrating cul de sac, he spent a year of respite in Switzerland where he resolved to throw everything he had left into poetry. However, when news of Susette Gontard's death in 1802 reached him, he became distraught and suffered the first pangs of the insanity which would see him later sequestered in the Tübingen Tower. Following treatment, he continued writing sporadically and held a position as court librarian in Homburg. In 1805, Hölderlin, a staunch supporter of the French Revolution, joined Jacobin militants led by his friend Isaac von Sinclair in a futile conspiracy against the Elector of Württemberg. He was accused of high treason but released as being mentally unfit to stand trial. With his behaviour spiralling out of control, he entered a clinic attached to the University of Tübingen, and was deemed incurable. A year later he was discharged and given at most three years of life. It was then that the kindly carpenter Ernst Zimmer stepped up to the plate and offered to care for the fallen poet in the tower room above his workshop on the Neckar. This turreted tower had once formed part of the old fortifications of the city and Hölderlin was to spend the next thirty-six years of his life there until his death in 1843. Today the tower is known as the Hölderlinturm and can be visited. It houses the archive of the Hölderlin Society. During his time in the tower Hölderlin wrote a new, simpler, direct form of poetry and played the piano, often monotonously, with his famously uncut fingernails clattering up and down the keys, to visitors' astonishment. He became something of a spectacle in Tübingen, verging on an exhibit in a freak show, for passing travellers and curiosity seekers. None of his family ever visited him nor showed the slightest interest in his well-being, merely shamelessly bickering over his inheritance. His former colleagues abandoned him, Hegel and Schelling vanished from the scene and at his funeral there were no mourners save for the Zimmer family.

After an initial period of obscurity following his death, the late-nineteenth and twentieth centuries saw Hölderlin's legacy consolidate to become one of the cornerstones of German literature. Hölderlin's drawn-out period in the tower meant that he had become severed from the literary affairs of his time and was forgotten, despite the efforts of friends to keep his work alive. Nietzsche saw in Hölderlin's poetry, and especially *Hyperion*, a fellow venerator of the Greeks, a herald of freedom of thought and life affirmation viewed through the prism of high cultural achievement. The mature poems influenced later poets and writers such as Rilke, Trakl, Hesse and Stefan George, yet the finely cut gems of shorter verse such as the famous 'Half of Life' also have their followers. The poet Paul Celan for one was strongly influenced by the later poems and fragments Hölderlin penned in the tower, works which were originally written off as mere expressions of mental atrophy. But it is not only poets who have been powerfully moved by the works of Hölderlin: thinkers such as Heidegger, Adorno, Derrida and Foucault owe a great debt to him, as do composers who have set his work to music. Of these the most prominent are Brahms, Strauss, Hindemith, Britten, Orff, Ligeti and Reger, but there are many others. In more recent years Hölderlin's extraordinary life story and curious existence closeted in the tower has also attracted a number of visual artists and film and television directors. The works of Hölderlin continue to be translated and re-translated into countless languages across the world.